How to ReBuild Trust and Let Go of Resentment

Start to Regain Trust in Your Relationship Today

by Anne Bridges

Table of Contents

Introduction

It is no secret that trust is the foundation of what makes any relationship work. Trust is known to be the fundamental basis of intimacy and love. When trust is lost, with it goes security, safety, love, friendship, and respect – it is often replaced with insecurity, anger, fear, anxiety, and resentment; the aggrieved party becomes like the police, the CIA and/or an FBI agent.

Distrust causes husbands/wives/partners to start looking through text messages, emails and asking countless questions such as *"who were you talking to and where on earth have you been for 5 whole minutes?"* Life becomes filled with consistent arguments – small and big – about what is actually going on, instead of taking what is spoken at face value.

The most experienced marriage or couple therapist will agree that there is no thornier subject than the betrayal or loss of trust, regardless of the form it may take. Most times, the aggrieved person is not mad that he or she was lied to; they are more hurt and upset that now, they cannot trust the other party again.

Have you lost the trust of your partner and you want to win it back? Or has someone betrayed your trust and you really want to learn to trust them again? The question that may be going through your head is *"can you restore romantic or sexual trust once it has been destroyed or broken?"* Well, it is possible although sometimes difficult, as betrayal cannot be erased at the snap of a finger. It will take some time.

The silver lining is that the aftermath of betrayal offers you and your partner the chance to reinforce your relationship and live a happier life together. If you and your partner honestly talk about what happened, the two of you will open up a pathway to a deeper level of intimacy. Although you cannot be a hundred percent positive that you will not be betrayed again, you sure can minimize the chances.

Do not wait to get help concerning your trust issues! Because mistrust can take root and become a part and parcel of your person. You do not want to be THAT PERSON who suspects everyone because someone dear to your heart once betrayed your trust. Once you know how to build/re-build trust, you can gradually start trusting your partner.

Chapter 1: What is Trust?

Trust is simply the willingness to unguardedly interact with someone. This simply means you leave yourself open to the person that you trust because you strongly believe that they will not cause you any harm. Trust is something that is reciprocal – this means when a person gives their trust, the other person receives it and then returns it.

Being able to trust your partner wholeheartedly clearly shows that you care for him or her; it also makes it obvious that you value their independence and what makes them unique.

Having Trouble Trusting?

It is really hard for a person to trust you if you are not willing to trust them. It is important to understand that trust also involves some level of risk, if you wait for a period of time when you feel that there is no risk in a relationship, then (quite naturally) you will never trust. It is of utmost importance that you are smart about who you extend your trust to and how much trust you allow yourself to give them. If your partner has betrayed your trust once, you should not be too afraid to learn to trust again, especially if they are sorry for betraying your trust and are willing to change.

Have You Betrayed the Trust of Your Partner?

Okay, there is no easy way to say this – if you have betrayed the trust of your man or woman, and you want to get back their trust, you have to understand that you may never get back their trust one hundred percent. There, we have said it.

People who have been betrayed often put up strong defences. They kind of have barbed wires and other emotional security threat deterrents around their hearts. In other words, they would think twice about trusting anyone again. So, you will need to be prepared to put in the work (a lot of it) to win back their trust again.

Incomplete Trust

One thing is for certain, no one can turn back the hands of time. You and your partner may not feel the same way about each other again – trust has been damaged, and like Humpty Dumpty, it is hard to put back together again. As the two of you work together to put your relationship back on track, the two of you may see each other differently. What may be going through your mind could be, "*Maybe I can trust him/her again, but from henceforth I will need to be extra careful*". Your trust level will not be as complete as it once was, you may experience any of the following types of incomplete trust:

- **Guarded Trust**: What may be going through your mind could be "I will trust you again, but I will be on the lookout for another treachery. If you could do this once, who says it may not happen again? So, I will be on guard and therefore not be taken by surprise next time."

- **Conditional Trust:** What may be going through your mind could be "I will trust you again but you will need to meet my conditions, like if you do not interact with the accomplice again."

- **Selective Trust:** What may be going through your mind could be "I will trust you with the household expenses but not with raw cash. You can use debit cards to continue to shop for the household supplies as you have done in the past. But I will require receipts for every purchase you make and frequent reassurance that you have stopped gambling."

When you make any of the aforementioned agreements, this means that you are doing the right thing – you are taking the first giant step in the right direction.

What If You Cannot Restore Trust?

Suppose it is not possible to restore trust? There are times when you feel like you can never trust anyone ever again. If your spouse/partner whom you love dearly breaks the trust you had in them, it is not helpful to focus on what happened and choose to NEVER trust anyone again. You would end up making life too difficult for yourself if you choose to live a life where you are constantly suspicious of others. While you are well aware of the dangers of trusting others too quickly, do not obsess. Even if a part of you screams "Watch Out!" It is good to give others the benefit of the doubt before trusting them completely.

Chapter 2: What Breaks Trust in a Relationship?

A person who is untrustworthy basically hurts his or her relationship with not only their significant other, but their relationships with other people as well.

Here are the common ways to break trust in a relationship:

1. Telling Lies

Most relationships end because the other party was not being entirely honest – any relationship built on a lie or a bed of lies will definitely collapse once the truth comes out. Lies of omission are types of lies which deliberately attempt to deceive the other person by intentionally omitting portions of the truth. A lie is often told to cover up the perpetrator's misdeeds or to give the other party's a false impression and attempt to influence the other party's behavior by omitting vital details.

For example, if you lied about your age the first time you met your partner, it may not seem like a big deal. But, the moment your partner finds out that you lied about something as basic as your age after you have both been dating for a couple of months, he or she would begin to wonder what else you have been lying to them about. Your partner may feel that you may also be lying about how much you make, how healthy you are etc. They may also begin to start running every single conversation they have had with you through their head in order to pick out any lies they think you might have told them about yourself.

People find it difficult to trust anyone who has been caught in a lie. Can you imagine the impact of lies on a family when the liar is actually the head of the family? Telling lies is definitely one of the most common ways to break trust.

2. Failing to Walk the Talk

Everyone knows that *"Talk is Cheap,"* but rather the action that you demonstrate helps your partner trust you. You will break trust if you fail to clearly demonstrate the behavioral expectations; in other words if you do not *"Practice What You Preach."* Think about it, would you trust a person who talks about the horrors of corruption, and find out that the person is actually a corrupt official? No one trusts a person who talks about one thing and does the exact opposite of what he or she speaks about.

14

3. Failing to Keep Promises

It is always important to do what you say you are going to do. Reliable, dependable, and consistent behavior is definitely at the heart of building trust. It is very irritating to deal with people who never follow through on the commitments they make. Failing to keep your promise is one sure way to destroy your partner's trust. Be on time, make that phone call, it sounds far easy enough; sadly, these commonsense basics are most times the basic things that we fail to do. When you keep the promises you make, you will no doubt encourage trust to grow.

4. Cheating

It is no secret that, across the entire world, cheating is the number one reason why people stop trusting their spouse or partner. A cheating spouse/partner is often perceived to be a liar as well – this is because a cheating spouse will also lie in order to cover up his or her affair. For example, when a cheating spouse receives a phone call from his or her lover, and their significant other walks into the room, they immediately act as though they are talking to someone else such as a relative, a close friend, a co-worker etc. Cheating is not only known to destroy trust, it has been known to be the number one reason why marriages end up in divorce.

Quite honestly, it is often difficult - bordering on nearly impossible – to entirely forgive and trust a partner who cheated. Most people (especially women) do not want to be put in a position where they start to do any of the following:

- Look through phone logs

- Read text messages on their spouse/partner's cell phone

- Hack into their spouse/partner's twitter or Facebook account

- Read their spouse/partner's email messages

- Be suspicious of why the spouse/partner is returning from work late

- Ask questions about where their partner has been, who he has been with, and what were they doing?

- Nag their spouse/partner

- And basically freak out at the thought of re-living the whole cheating episode all over again.

16

Please Note:

Most people want to know if a romantic or sexual trust can be restored when lost, damaged, or destroyed? Well, yes, it is possible. But as mentioned earlier, no one gets past disloyalty overnight, it will take some time and effort.

According to statistics, unlike women, men find it a lot harder to forgive and trust a spouse or partner who cheated on them.

5. Money Mismanagement

Believe it or not, mismanagement of finances can destroy trust. For example, if a man or woman trusts his or her significant other with their combined money, only to discover that the money for groceries, mortgage, bills etc has been used to fund a bad habit such as gambling, drugs etc. this can definitely lead to trust issues. No one wants to trust a "waster" with their financial substance. A lot of couples have had to work through money mismanagement issues.

6. Divulging Information Shared in Confidence

One of the most horrible things you can do to destroy your partner's trust is to divulge secrets shared with you in confidence. "*Diarrhoea of the mouth*" is something that no honorable person should ever be accused of. Sharing very important information with your partner simply shows that you love, respect, and trust the person. A person who goes around divulging information shared with him or her in total confidence is killing their partner's trust.

Chapter 3: Why is Trust Important in a Relationship?

Having trust in a relationship is certainly a must. When there is trust, with it comes security and freedom to experience the complete potential of love, vulnerability, and intimacy the relationship has to offer. When there is no trust, there is insecurity and fear, which dampens and limits the relationship's potential.

It is very important to understand that when you trust your partner or spouse, there is freedom to share your soul and your heart with him or her – this is because you are aware in your mind and spirit that what you share will be treasured and valued. Trust offers you the opportunity to keep adding building block after building block to the foundation of your relationship; therefore constructing a studier platform where the two of you can weather life's storms together.

If trust has not been established and maintained before heading straight for the marriage altar, you will be setting yourself for a future with "doom" written all over it. If you build your marriage on a poorly constructed foundation, you will experience a painful and difficult journey to a blissful marriage. The need for complete trust permeates every area of marriage –

intimacy, communication, finances, spirituality, judgement etc – there is simply no way you can ignore the presence of trust or its lack thereof. Without trust, you can only expect misunderstanding, pain, stress, and argument.

Broken trust in a marriage can be devastating and even harder to get past. There is still hope for loss of trust in a relationship. The biggest things to keep in mind are:

- The "Offender" must be totally committed to changing his or her behavior in order to win back the trust that has been broken or destroyed.

- The "Aggrieved" must be totally committed to forgive and should understand that there is nothing the "Offender" can do to undo the harm that they have done, and that the process of building/rebuilding trust will possibly take a lot of time, patience, and maybe professional help.

Trust is truly a key component to a relationship. It is something that is woven into the fiber of all aspects of a relationship. Trust is something that should be enjoyed and protected. There is no doubt that trust is a must in a relationship, without it, the relationship does not stand a chance.

Chapter 4: Effective Ways of Building/Re-Building Trust in Your Relationship

When you discover that the one you love has broken your trust, instead of having a meltdown, you should take a few minutes to sit down with your partner to have a discussion with him or her on why the whole thing happened. Next, take some time off to clear your head – you should not just give up on the relationship you have spent a lot of time building. You may feel really hurt and think that you no longer have the capacity to trust, but trust can be rebuilt, especially if the offending party has proven to be otherwise loyal to you all the period you have known them; all you need to do is to find what will work for you.

Reports of infidelity, IRS scandals, misuse of finances etc all lead to mistrust. As mentioned earlier, trust is the foundation of any relationship. Trust basically involves 3 components:

1. Integrity
2. Honesty
3. Justice

A relationship flourishes when there is trust, and without it, the relationship is headed straight for the rocks. So, what are the effective ways to build trust in a relationship, particularly if that trust has been lost or damaged?

Here are 10 effective ways to build/re-build trust:

1. Admit to Your Mistake

If you are the "Offender" you will need to admit to your errors if you want to re-gain your partner's trust. Admitting to the mistakes you have made is one of the most important trust re-building steps. Why? It simply shows that you are humble and sincere when you own up to the mistakes you have made. It shows your partner that you respect him or her enough to be upfront and honest. When you show some vulnerability, it goes a long way in rebuilding trust. Take responsibility and do not try to downplay your actions. Remember, it takes a long time to build trust, and yet only a moment to damage it.

2. Be Genuinely Sorry

If you broke your partner's trust, your remorse must be evidenced. If you show no signs of remorse, your partner will still doubt you, which could lead to the breakup of your relationship. You do not want your partner to think that you are not sorry for what you did, but only sorry that you got caught (assuming that you were caught in the act).

3. Be Open to Answering Your Partner's Questions

The moment that trust is broken, the aggrieved person should be free to ask you questions in order to make sense of what happened. The offender should not complain about having to provide answers to uncomfortable questions that his or her partner might ask. Questions such as:

- How much money did you steal from me?

- How many times did you sleep with him/her?

- Do you love him/her?

- Why did you do it?

- Please tell me how "it" happened, I want a blow by blow account

4. Forgive

If you are the offended party, you should forgive the person who betrayed your trust. This does not mean that you condone the actions of the person, play down the impact, or simply act like it never happened. Forgiveness also means that you acknowledge the breach of trust and you have made up your mind not to allow it to fester in bitterness and unforgiveness. Being able to forgive your partner is just the first step. Forgiving your partner also means not throwing their offense back in their face any chance you get.

5. Give Assurance

You will need to give assurance where and when it is needed if you are the offending party. A lot of reassurance is required in order to help your partner see all the efforts that you are making.

6. Have Some Empathy

If you are working towards regaining lost trust, you will need to be empathetic to the pain that you must have caused your partner. Most times, people want to admit to the mistakes that they have made and then move on with their life without any consequences. However, pain is typically involved here and will require some time to work through. As the offender, you will need to be empathetic to the period that it would take your partner to heal and be ready again to give it another try.

7. Be Patient

It is important to understand that you cannot hurry the re-building of violated trust. It takes time for the other party to figure out if your relationship is worth salvaging.

8. Never Use Your Partner's Past Indiscretion as a Weapon

It may sound pretty harsh, but the truth is that what is done is done. As the offended party, your main focus is to move forward. Yes, there are times when you will remember how your partner betrayed your trust, but the pain will definitely go away. Do not keep bringing up the past and use it as an excuse to fight with your partner.

9. Do Not Keep Secrets

Any relationship that is built on secrets never ends up well. One of the major ingredients to building a healthy relationship is honesty, even if it hurts both you and your partner to be honest with each other.

10. Work Towards Reconciliation

It takes one person to forgive and it takes two to reconcile. It is tough to throw away the many years you have invested in building your relation. Do not be too quick to throw all that emotional, financial, and spiritual investment away without even giving the situation a second thought. Give the offender a chance to explain what happened before you make up your mind to put an end to your relationship, you may be surprised to know that the situation is not as bad as you thought it was.

Chapter 5: The Dos and Don'ts of Building (or Re-Building) Trust in Your Relationship

As mentioned earlier, no relationship will stand a chance if it is not built on trust. There are dos and don'ts of building/re-building trust in relationships.

Do Ensure that You Communicate with Your Partner

It is important to communicate with your partner, because communication is a strong component needed in building a successful relationship. When you are in the early stages of building your relationship, you and your partner are basically trying to get to know each other in order to figure out how you can make your relationship grow strong. Communicating with your partner is pertinent to helping him or her understand your person and what you want and need from the relationship. It is of the utmost importance to listen to your partner whenever they are communicating with you. He or she will certainly appreciate the attention you give them and will feel your commitment to helping the relationship flourish.

Being honest also goes hand-in-hand with communication. Dishonesty is the bullet that kills any relationship. Even an insignificant lie can begin to raise doubts in the mind of your partner. Holding back information from your partner is definitely a trust killer - although it may not be lying in theory, but it might make your partner begin to wonder what else you are withholding.

Do Try Not To Be Someone Else – Be Yourself!

When you like someone a lot, the first instinct is to ensure that you put your best foot forward. However, it is really hard to keep maintaining the façade. When you present your "TRUE" self from the get-go, your partner will recognize that you are not being someone else and will reciprocate by not holding back his or her real personality.

Do Keep the Promises that You Make

This is perhaps one of the most important ways to build trust. You should be a person who is known for keeping his or her word. When you make a promise and you follow through, you will be perceived as a dependable person. Your partner will feel more secure knowing that you can be relied upon if something happens. You will notice that your partner will make a great effort to ensure that he/she does the same for you.

Do Support the Activities of Your Partner

Be supportive when it comes to your partner's projects, endeavors etc. If you do not like fashion shows, but want to support your partner's dreams of becoming a fashion designer; you should look for other ways to be supportive. Try dropping off and picking up your partner from fashion shows or seminars in order to support your partner. By making a good effort to support your partner, you are showing that you care for him or her while being honest about your own person.

Don't Embarrass Your Partner

If you find that you have been drawn into a disagreement between your partner and someone else, and you internally disagree with your partner, you should take a neutral position while in front of others, and then talk about the matter later with your partner in private. When you keep things between the two of you, you will show him or her that you respect him/her as a person instead of embarrassing him/her while both of you are out; which will definitely make matters a lot worse.

Don't Nag Your Partner

You need to understand that no one is perfect – that's right, this includes you. If you detest being nagged, think about how your partner would feel if you nag him or her. Your partner wants to feel that he or she is in a relationship with a grownup. Trust that your partner is not intentionally trying to get you upset. If something constantly keeps coming up, and it bothers you, you should talk to him or her in order to figure out a solution that the two of you can live with.

Don't Air Your Grievances While You Are Still Mad

The simplest way to destroy the trust that you have built from scratch in your relationship is to encourage arguments when your emotions are high. Airing a grievance in the heat of the moment is certainly the riskiest thing you can do in your relationship. It is better to sleep on the matter instead of allowing your emotions to flood and end up not solving anything. When you sleep on the matter, you will wake up with a clearer understanding of what happened.

Don't Make a Habit of Assuming the Worst

One of the things that you can do to build trust in your relationship is to never assume the worst of your man or woman. To build trust, you have to show your partner that you strongly believe their trustworthiness. If you notice patterns of behavior in your partner that may have sent your red flags up, then talk to your partner. You should tell him or her how you feel and work on finding a mutual agreement. Your partner may not even realize that he or she is doing something that you are not comfortable with.

Don't Be Too Serious

You should take time to laugh with your partner, and you should also not have any problems laughing at yourself. Laughing will help you to diffuse the conflicts in your relationships. By choosing to diffuse conflict, you are simply learning to trust the perspective of each other. Laughter does not only reduce stress, it can also help bring you and your partner a little closer.

Let's face it, building trust in a relationship is not exactly as easy as it may seem. You are basically opening your heart to another person, and this type of vulnerability is quite difficult. Building trust sure takes time. You should give your partner time to figure out how to offer you the support and love that you need by also being honest and supportive as well.

Remember, you are only in a relationship because you want to be, and not because you are doing your partner a favor.

Chapter 6: How Trust is Created

Okay, most people don't know this but ***trust is a choice***. Although there are no ironclad guarantees that you will never experience another betrayal, you do have the power to create a trusting romantic relationship. The moment you meet a person, you can start to intentionally nurture trust. This is the part where you say "How?"

- You will need to be in integrity with who you are

- Know your real feelings and needs so that you can disclose them to your partner

- If you are true to yourself, you will be true to others

- Know exactly who you are and what you want in a relationship

- If you tell others the whole truth, without withholding information, they tend to reciprocate

- Trust your own instincts to alert you to any dishonesty, rather than trying to actively seek it out or uncover it on your own

Choose a person who is worthy of your trust – think about it, would you want to date a man who is a notorious womanizer and think you can trust him not to cheat on you? Allow your intuition (also known as gut instincts) to guide you. If your gut says a big fat "NO!" be sure to heed it.

Be sure to watch and listen attentively. If you perceive any signs of danger, such as broken promises or little white lies, pay attention to them. A person who is not worthy of anyone's trust is not going to change overnight even if you would be a great influence over them.

You will need to create trust moment-by-moment. Each time an issue arises, when you feel that your trust is being violated, you should endeavor to talk about it. Doing this may make the two of you quite uncomfortable at first, but it is sure to bring the two of you closer in the long run.

Do not hesitate to ask serious questions such as:

- Where were you last night when I called and got no answer?

- Who was the lady who left your apartment this morning?

40

- Why were you a few hours late for our meeting with your friends?

- Who does this nail polish on your dresser belong to?

If you feel that something is not quite right, you are probably right. Learn to follow your intuition.

Conclusion

There are times when it feels really difficult to open your heart to anyone again after someone in your past violated your trust. But you cannot enjoy life if you choose to a live it while not trusting your significant other. Remember the law of attraction, if you think your partner will violate your trust, then prepare to live with trust issues for the rest of your life. To build trust, you must open yourself – this includes the good, the bad, and the ugly side of you.

If you have broken the trust of your partner, there is still a ray of hope to regain his or her trust. But you will need to be prepared to work hard to win back the trust you lost.

If someone violated your trust, you can learn to trust them again – just give yourself the opportunity to trust again, especially if the person is worth a second chance.

Made in the USA
Monee, IL
18 February 2022

91455480R00028